Original title:
Finding Purpose in the Quiet Moments

Copyright © 2025 Creative Arts Management OÜ
All rights reserved.

Author: Franklin Stone
ISBN HARDBACK: 978-1-80566-205-1
ISBN PAPERBACK: 978-1-80566-500-7

Starlit Thoughts in Solitude

Under stars, my mind does race,
As I ponder my sock's missing face.
Grilling up dreams in a cosmic chair,
Wondering if aliens really care.

With a comet's tail for a cozy quilt,
Pondering life while my coffee's spilt.
Juggling planets like a circus clown,
In the stillness, I'm the king, not the town.

When Time Pauses

Tick-tock goes the silly clock,
Counting minutes like a nervous rock.
I muse on how to make a cake,
And end up with a kitten named Drake.

Time halts as I look at my phone,
Finding new memes that I've never known.
Laughter bubbles like a soda pop,
In these moments, I can never stop.

Inward Journeys Amidst the Noise

In a cacophony of random tweets,
I search for wisdom in dancing beats.
A squirrel in my head throws a rave,
While the cat is busy being brave.

Listening close as chaos swirls,
I draft a plot where penguins twirl.
Amidst the yells, a whisper comes,
Telling me to follow the crumbs.

The Serenity of Letting Go

I drop my worries like old shoes,
And kick back like it's time to snooze.
With a laugh, I let my thoughts drift by,
Chasing clouds and a butterfly.

Unraveling dreams like a knotted thread,
Searching for crumbs I haven't fed.
As the world rushes, I dance in place,
Embracing the calm with a funny face.

Echoing Heartbeats

In the stillness, a thought's little dance,
A heart's psalm, in its own trance.
Counting sheep? Oh what a bore!
Try counting snacks; you'll crave more!

Whispers of dreams, they tickle my ear,
Like popcorn popping, it's all very clear.
When life goes quiet, the giggles arise,
Tickling the brain, much to my surprise.

The Light Behind Closed Eyes

Close your eyes, it's a hibernation,
What's that? A wild imagination!
Maybe a unicorn waltzes by,
Or a dancing potato, oh my!

The sunbeam sneaks beneath the door,
Inviting me to explore and soar.
In the dark, I hear the giggles,
Of dreams performing their little wiggles.

Meditation in Motion

Twist and turn, like spaghetti on a fork,
Meditation? More like a quirky cork!
One minute zen, the next a sneeze,
Suddenly pondering how to please the bees!

Inhale deep, then do a little jig,
Calm in chaos, like a dancing pig.
Silly thoughts float around like balloons,
In this circus, I'm the clown who croons.

Chasing Fleeting Tranquility

I chase the calm, with a comedic stride,
Tripping over thoughts like they're bubblegum wide.
Why is silence so tricky to catch?
Like a cat with a laser—oh, so mismatched!

In stillness, giggles peek out to play,
Like socks that vanish on laundry day.
Let's ride the waves of this playful quest,
In this quiet chaos, I find my best!

Echoes of Inner Harmony

In the silence, socks do dance,
Chasing lint like true romance.
A spoon hums a catchy tune,
As the cat plots to steal my spoon.

Amidst the chaos, tea grows cold,
While I ponder mysteries untold.
The clock ticks like a silly tune,
As I search for my lost shoe too.

Gentle Shifts in the Soft Light

Sunbeams play on my weary face,
As I trip on a shoelace.
The toaster pops with cheeky glee,
While I sing off-key to my tea.

Breezes whisper secrets low,
To plants outside that dance and grow.
A squirrel stares from yonder tree,
Judging my dancing, wild and free.

Serene Footprints of Time

Time wobbles like a jelly mold,
While I search for jokes untold.
Leaves rustle, eager to conspire,
As I struggle not to tire.

A snail races, oh what a sight,
Competing in this daily fight.
With quiet giggles, I engage,
In the rhythmic dance of this stage.

Whispers from the Edge of Existence

Between the whispers of the breeze,
I glimpse a dance of carefree bees.
They tumble, buzz, and say, 'Hooray!'
While I contemplate lunch today.

In the stillness, cookies burn,
As I toss and twist and turn.
A moment's bliss, a harmless prank,
With crumbs to sweep and no time to thank.

The Art of Slowing Down

In a world that rushes fast,
I stop to stare at a passing snail.
He's got life figured out, I swear,
While I trip over my own shoelace tale.

Tea takes ages, that's no lie,
But watch it steep, oh what a show!
Like a sitcom brewed by the sky,
Where time just laughs, 'Take it slow!'

Counting clouds can be a task,
Especially when I lose track,
One's a dinosaur, or maybe a flask?
Oh look, there's the kitchen rack.

The clock mocks me with every tick,
I ponder why I'm in such a rush,
But the pizza's cold, that's the trick,
Guess I'll eat it in a quiet hush.

Moments Wrapped in Stillness

In moments where the world stands still,
I trip on thoughts like hidden stones.
Each pause unravels a zany thrill,
As I converse with my garden gnomes.

Sipping tea with cheese on toast,
Who knew a snack's a wise advisor?
Even my cat looks like she's engrossed,
In the art of perfect daydream riser.

Birds gossip above in their cheery way,
What's on the menu, who brings the seeds?
My eavesdropping's crafted in delightful play,
Nature's whispers—celebrate their needs!

Where Dreams Steep

In a teacup swirls my Monday muse,
A splash of lemon, a sprinkle of hope.
Stirring joy from an afternoon snooze,
I ponder how tea makes a great dope.

Fluffy clouds hold secrets tight,
I challenge them to a showdown, right?
They laugh, 'We're soft, but in sunlight,
Your socks are more lost than we in flight.'

With each sip, my laughter's a riot,
Tea spills stories, just look at me go!
With every brew, this heart feels quiet,
Who knew tea could steal the show?

Breath of the Unobserved

In whispers of wind, I hear a call,
A shimmy of leaves—what do they know?
They gossip about the best of all,
While I awkwardly try to weave my flow.

The cat in the window nods with glee,
Onlookers, unaware of the grand play.
She breeds applause for a leaf on the tree,
While I take notes, pondering my sway.

Lawn chairs are where we dream aloud,
With rubber duckies guarding our quests.
In each wild moment lies laughter proud,
As careless bliss puts us to tests.

Unraveling the Threads of Stillness

In a world of buzzing gadgets,
I found peace under my bed,
There's more to life than hashtags,
Especially when you're getting fed.

Socks and dust bunnies collide,
In that glorious harmony of fluff,
Meditation? Nah, I just hide,
From adulting—it's way too tough.

Quiet moments twist and bend,
Like spaghetti twirling on a fork,
Laughter sparks as thoughts descend,
In the calm, I dance and cork.

So here's my secret, eh, it's clear,
In silence, I let my dreams take flight,
While savoring that last slice of pizza,
Who knew chill-time could feel so right?

The Mosaic of Silent Moments

I sip my tea, oh what a sight,
The kettle sings, it's quite profound,
But curious cat wants in on the bite,
Turns my zen into a circus ground.

Puzzles come alive at dusk,
Pieces scattered everywhere but here,
Finding joy in the mess, no fuss,
As I giggle with a touch of cheer.

Birds chime in with their song,
But my dog thinks it's a noise complaint,
He barks along, what could be wrong?
In silence, he's the loudest saint.

Each moment whispers, 'Take a break',
Like my plant—oh no, it's gone awry,
Yet in this stillness, I'll not forsake,
A chuckle blooms as I wave goodbye.

Shadows of Contemplation

In the realm of shadows, I ponder,
Like a sock left behind a chair,
Thoughts drift in and start to wander,
Right before I dye my hair.

Tick-tock goes the clock for fun,
Reminding me of bills I owe,
Yet laughter rolls in like the sun,
As I contemplate the way to flow.

I find wisdom in the fridge light,
As leftovers share their secrets old,
In the quiet hum, it feels so right,
To eat and smile, a sight to behold.

Oh, reflections shine in my tea cup,
Each sip a journey, what a thrill,
Thoughts race, my brain won't shut up,
Yet it's peaceful chaos, and I'm still.

The Glow of a Quiet Mind

Amidst the glow of evening's grace,
I chuckle at the laundry pile,
The chaos draped in a funny face,
A sock's escaped, let's stay awhile.

Silent nights and thought-bubbles rise,
Like my cat plotting world domination,
In this stillness, I hear the sighs,
Of missing spoons in the celebration.

Meditating with a bowl of chips,
Crunching thoughts, both bright and silly,
In every bite, a joke of flips,
Who knew quiet could feel so frilly?

So here's to laughter in shadows cast,
A glow ignites the thoughts confined,
In every moment, make it last,
With humor we dance, intertwined.

A Tapestry of Quietude

In silence blooms a crazy thought,
A squirrel dance that can't be bought.
With coffee brewing, my dog snorts loud,
While I concoct a plan to astound.

Each tick of the clock plays hide and seek,
As my cat channels her inner mystique.
I wonder if llamas get to dream,
Or is that just part of my morning scheme?

The toaster's jingle sings of toast,
A breakfast feast I love the most.
Yet underneath the buttered grin,
I ponder where the socks have been.

Oh, sweet serenity wrapped in jest,
Where chaos and calm put humor to the test.
In quirky moments, life's best grooves,
A tapestry woven that truly moves.

In the Company of Shadows

In shadows play my wacky dreams,
Of dancing eggs and ribboned beams.
The unyielding silence starts to speak,
With belly laughs and thoughts that sneak.

The couch a throne of funny quirks,
As dust bunnies plan their covert works.
With popcorn ready for a cheer,
I muse on where the remote did disappear.

A cat conspiracy brews at noon,
While I contemplate the taste of a spoon.
Does laughter echo when no one's around?
Or do echoes simply take a break now?

In odd little corners, silliness thrives,
With socks relocating to faraway drives.
A dance of the futile, caught in the glow,
In the company of shadows, thoughts overflow.

Harmonies of the Unheard

The fridge hums like a gentle muse,
In harmonious notes that I can't refuse.
As ice cubes clink a cheerful tone,
I ponder if my chair is overthrown.

Outside, a bird picks at its toes,
While I chase whims where imagination flows.
A tango with tangents, I follow the lead,
In silliness blossomed like topsy-turvy seed.

A fortune cookie's wisdom on my desk,
Suggests daringly I play a prank at the fest.
But who needs noise when the world feels bright?
In soft-spoken giggles the heart takes flight.

Oh, harmonies of whispers ripple the air,
Where even silence holds a flavor to share.
In moments retreating from hustle and fray,
I'll sip on laughter, come what may.

The Poetry of Pauses

The pause between laughter's uproar,
Where thoughts bounce gently, exploring the floor.
I trip on a shoe and gasp with glee,
While my coffee dreams of being more than just tea.

With crumbs of cookies dancing in air,
I muse on life – absurd but fair.
Will clouds wear pajamas at dusk's soft call?
Do owls have dreams? I could ponder it all.

The microwave sings like a balladeer,
In riveting rhythms, it draws me near.
Each beep a reminder that I must abide,
While my snack breaks into a comedic slide.

In playful pauses, the universe winks,
With mirth dancing around in lovely blinks.
So, here's to the joy in stillness embraced,
In the poetry of pauses, let laughter be traced.

Beneath the Surface of Chaos

In the chaos, there's a dance,
A jiggle here, a wobbly prance.
Coffee spills, but hey, who cares?
The laundry's talking, it has layers.

My cat thinks she's a graceful queen,
Chasing shadows, looking quite mean.
Thunder roars like a cosmic joke,
While I giggle, trying not to choke.

A sock escapes—oh, where'd it roam?
It's journeying far, far from home.
As kids build forts from random stuff,
I sit back, saying, 'Life's enough!'

In bed, the silence is a prank,
Thoughts are swimming in a sweet tank.
Chaos reigns, but oh so fun,
In this mess, the heart has won!

Lullabies of the Mind

A snore escapes like a gentle breeze,
Whispers of dreams are sure to tease.
Pillows fighting for a cozy spot,
In this pillow war, we're all distraught.

Thoughts dance lightly, on tiptoe bright,
Worry waltzes, but that's alright.
While socks slip off and minds drift away,
We're composing lullabies for the day.

A list of chores gets lost in air,
Dusted dreams float, here and there.
'Tomorrow' giggles from the shelf,
As I navigate my inner elf.

In quiet moments, laughter blooms,
Finding joy amidst the rooms.
The world outside may spin and shout,
But in my head, it's a funny bout!

The Beauty of Unhurried Moments

The clock ticks slow like a sleepy snail,
Coffee's brewing with a whimsical trail.
Mismatched socks give a knowing wink,
And my breakfast? Oh! It's more pink than ink!

A chair creaks softly, sharing tales,
Of moments lost on forgotten trails.
The cat, the sofa—what's in between?
A legend lives where the dust bunnies preen.

Outside, the world zooms by in haste,
While I nibble a muffin, slow-paced.
Savor the silence, let laughter spark,
Embrace the chaos, don't miss the mark.

Breathe in the calm, it's a funny show,
In unhurried spaces, creativity flows.
Turning chaos into a silly art,
In the slow lane, I find my heart!

Hidden Treasures of Repose

Underneath that pile of clothes,
A mystery brews where no one knows.
Quirky socks in a cheeky fight,
While the cat prepares for her nightly flight.

The fridge hums tunes of yesteryears,
Reminding me of fish and cheers.
Everything old suddenly bright and new,
As I browse leftovers, pondering who's who.

In the bathtub, my thoughts take dips,
Bubbles giggle, on the edge of ships.
Conversations with rubber ducks abound,
In the solitude, pure joy is found.

In downtime, the laughter sneaks,
Tickles the soul, where the heart speaks.
Embrace the weird, let silliness grow,
For treasure lies in the unhurried flow!

Glimmers of Inner Light

In the still of the night, I hear my mind,
Like a squirrel on a quest, in search of a find.
It dances around thoughts, chasing its tail,
Trying to uncover the cheese in the grail.

With a grand cup of tea, I ponder my fate,
Seeking epiphanies while snacking on cake.
The kettle whistles loud, a siren's sweet call,
As I scribble my dreams on the back of the wall.

A cat might join in, with a yawn so profound,
Reminding me softly to take leaps, not bound.
Together we sit, as wild ideas spin,
In the quiet chaos, a chuckle within.

Every little moment, a joke in disguise,
Like tripping on shoelaces or saying goodbyes.
But amid all the laughter, the silliness flows,
There's a spark of delight that nobody knows.

The Pulse of Stillness

As I sit with a snack that I shouldn't have made,
The crinkles of chips serenade my charade.
Thoughts stumble like toddlers, unsteady and round,
In the silence, a giggle is all that I've found.

My dog snores away, a true philosopher,
Dreaming of squirrels, or perhaps he's a star.
We chat in our heads, as the seconds tick by,
No one else around, just a pie in the sky.

In the midst of this calm, a sneeze breaks the peace,
A chorus of laughter makes worries release.
Joy bubbles up quick, like soda in glass,
In the moments of stillness, the giggles amass.

Together we wander through thoughts and through dreams,
Frolicking lightly, like sun on the streams.
In the quiet, we find joy hidden in smiles,
While munching on snacks and gathering piles.

Solace Found in the Unsaid

In moments of hush, there's a riddle to mime,
With a wink and a nudge, we dance out of time.
The neighbors might wonder, what's causing the fuss,
But secrets are shared in our quietest hush.

I'll wave at the moon, as it winks back at me,
Throwing shadows like ghosts, a comical spree.
Each blink of the starlight is full of a jest,
Whispering laughs from a celestial quest.

Unsaid conversations are crowded with glee,
Like grabbing your shoelaces while setting them free.
In the echoes of silence, the giggles abound,
As we savor the quiet, our joy all around.

It's more than mere whispers; it's a chuckling sound,
With a sprinkle of mischief hidden all around.
In the embrace of the stillness, we find the refrain,
To laugh loud and hard, like we're losing the chain.

Timelessness in the Present

In the now, the clock has decided to pause,
Embracing the stillness, without any cause.
Every tick seems a giggle, a wink of the day,
While I munch on snacks and just let thoughts play.

I spy a dust mote doing ballet in light,
It pirouettes gracefully, what a curious sight!
With a whirl and a spin, it steals the grand show,
While outside, the world just continues to flow.

A whisper of laughter escapes from my soul,
As I try to calculate how many chips roll.
In the laughter of crumbs, I find solace anew,
In the silence, there's joy like a rabbit in view.

With each tiny moment, I flip through the scenes,
Of cats in the sun and sweet sprightly beans.
In the heart of the quiet, there's mischief to find,
As I chuckle along with the thoughts intertwined.

In the Pockets of Time

In the corner of my couch, I sit,
With crumbs of yesterday's snacks, a perfect fit.
Dreams tripping over each other, oh such a race,
While socks hide from shoes, in a comical place.

The clock ticks slowly, a snail on the wall,
Each second whispers secrets, then starts to sprawl.
I sip my tea, it splashes, whoops!
Better mop it up, before it forms new troops.

I ponder my life, as I pluck a hair,
Ocean of purpose? Nah, it's just a bear.
Turns out my cat's judgment is rather grand,
She's the queen of this quiet, with a whispering band.

With laughter like bubbles, I float on my chair,
Time's sticky notes flutter, nothing else compares.
In the pockets of moments, I find a snack too,
Purpose may nap here, but so do cats, who knew?

Murmurs of the Heart's Desire

In the garden of thoughts, I dig a small hole,
What blooms is a joke, that tickles the soul.
My plant started dancing, what a sight to behold,
With petals like giggles, and stories untold.

A bee buzzes by, with a swagger so grand,
It whispers sweet nothings, while sippin' on bland.
Together we scheme, oh what a delight,
To turn this dull patch into a wild flight.

The sun casts a grin, on my wandering path,
As I trip over daisies, not counting the math.
Each stumble a chuckle, each pause a thought,
And even the weeds seem to bloom, quite unbought.

With whispers of worries, I wave them goodbye,
For laughter's my compass, beneath the big sky.
In murmurs of joy, I wade through my days,
Collecting the quirks like soft, silly rays.

Poetry of the Unseen

In shadows of silence, the quirks come alive,
A goblin of giggles knows just how to thrive.
It plays peek-a-boo with my thoughts as they glide,
In the poetry written where snickers reside.

The cat in the corner, a furry sage's touch,
Seems to know the secrets, oh my, so much!
As I ponder my meaning, she yawns and just stares,
Like she's the wise oracle, of carpets and chairs.

A sock on the floor dreams of wild escapades,
While fruit flies engage in invisible parades.
Where nonsense is noted and chaos dances free,
I find my own rhythm in this nonsense spree.

In the abstract moments, where laughter can sway,
The beauty of silence becomes my ballet.
With poetry hidden in every small scene,
Life's giggles remind me of what truly is keen.

Threads of Softness

Amidst the cushions, a podcast of sighs,
Each thread weaves a story, as daylight complies.
The sofa's a ship, sailing sea of my mind,
With pillows as crew, and snacks well-defined.

In this world of plush laughter, I find a soft nook,
Pouring my tea, while snacking on a book.
Pages flip gently, like whispers of dreams,
As the cat steals the thunder, or so it seems.

I scale the high mountains of laundry piled high,
Wondrous landscapes of garments that wave and sigh.
The dryer churns loudly; it sings like a bird,
Fabric soft tales, more amusing than heard.

Embracing this chaos, I balance and sway,
Finding lightness where seriousness lay.
In threads of absurdity, I stitch up my glee,
For in these small comforts, I'm wild and I'm free.

Whispers of the Still

In the stillness of my socks,
I once spoke with a box.
It replied with a clink,
Saying, 'Have you had a drink?'

A squirrel critiqued my tea,
Said it wasn't fancy enough for a bee.
I laughed as the sun made its show,
While learning from shadows below.

The cat gave me a squint,
As if judging my glint.
I told it, 'Don't you pout,
I'm just a human figure out!'

Breeze danced with my hair,
Claiming, 'Life's beyond compare.'
In these moments, I roam light,
Wit blooming like stars at night.

Beneath the Hush

Underneath the vast gray sky,
The ants threw a raucous pie.
They debated on flavors wide,
While I hid my chuckles outside.

A turtle slow-rolled in stride,
Laughing as the world tried to hide.
I asked it for sage advice,
It winked and said, 'Roll the dice!'

In corners where dust bunnies dwell,
I swear I heard the floor say, 'Well!'
'Got no time for a cleaning sweep,'
As the couch sighed, 'Let's just sleep!'

The clock ticked in slapstick tones,
Tick-tocking like the silliest drones.
In the hush, we find our glee,
Crafting humor quietly.

Solace in the Silence

In a moment, my sock drew a frown,
As if it wished it could wear a crown.
With banter so light, it took a stand,
Claiming it was a wanderer, unplanned.

The teapot burbled a chuckle,
Teasing me like a playful knuckle.
'Brew your dreams,' it chimed with cheer,
'Just don't serve them too near the deer!'

A couch potato whispered sweet,
'Life isn't so serious, take a seat.'
I giggled in respite from the race,
Finding joy in this funny space.

The walls laughed and echoed back,
Exchanging jokes in a silly knack.
In the stillness, the winks took flight,
Sharing giggles under moonlight.

Echoes of Introspection

In the echoes of my empty tea,
A goldfish winked, quite merrily.
It said, 'Go dust off your dreams!'
As it danced through the bubbles and beams.

The wall clock yawned with such flair,
'Why are you rushing when there's care?'
I chuckled, responding with wit,
'Time's just a funny little skit!'

My slippers schemed for a stroll,
'Let's venture and be on a roll!'
So we strolled through thoughts profound,
While cheeky pigeons clucked around.

In whispers of laughter, we learned to play,
Making friends with silence every day.
In moments so quiet, we dare to cheer,
Finding humor, the treasure near.

Moments That Fill the Void

In the silence, I stubbed my toe,
Wondering if life's dance is a toe-tapping show.
Coffee brews while socks swirl around,
In this chaos, meaning is humorously found.

The dog snored loud, a symphonic delight,
While I wrestled with snack time, a snack time fight.
A missed call rings, but I can't find my phone,
In the laughter of mishaps, I feel less alone.

With biscuits that crumble, and pillows that fluff,
Life's little blunders become the best stuff.
The irony's rich like a chocolate fondue,
Moments that fill gaps—who knew they would glue?

So I trip on a thought and burst into glee,
In the weirdest of moments, I find a me.
In each quirky pause, I feel a bit bold,
The jokes that the quiet moments have told.

Respite Between the Storms

Rain poured, then the sun waved hello,
I danced on puddles, the oddest of shows.
A squirrel with style, on my porch took a seat,
In the calm of the storm, life felt quite complete.

Life's faster than socks lost in the wash,
Yet here's a cozy nook, where thoughts bloom and squosh.
Baking adventures, a spoon slips and flies,
In sticky distractions, I uncover the wise.

Lightning's a show-off, but where's the punchline?
Clouds have their whispers, and raindrops their rhyme.
A moment of stillness, as wet dogs run wild,
Each laugh in the tempest feels like a child.

So in chaos we weave, threads of the funny,
Between gusts of laughter and mischief that's sunny.
I find joy in moments, in the eye of the fun,
Respite brings whimsy, and bestows me a pun.

The Essence of Softness

Couch cushions hug, like a cloud's warm embrace,
But finding the remote is life's great race.
With snacks on the floor and laughs in the air,
The softness is found in the absurdity there.

A cat perched high, judging my every move,
While I carefully plot my next snack attack groove.
They say silence speaks volumes, well, not in my street,
My chaos is quiet, where crazy and cozy meet.

Fluffy blankets and giggles blend well,
In thoughts like a marshmallow, I'm bound to excel.
In the spice of my life, I find cinnamon dreams,
Layered in laughter, it's funnier than it seems.

So here's to the moments, all silly and sweet,
In cushions of laughter, my heart finds its beat.
The essence of softness, a nest made of cheer,
In the stillness of giggles, I savor them here.

An Invitation to Be

Under the twinkling stars, I lost my last knish,
They rolled to a town where they grant three wishes.
While searching for snacks lost in the night,
I tripped over dreams—now that's quite a sight!

An owl hooted, giving me the side-eye,
Advising me gently 'Under the moon, just fly!'
The awkward ballet of me and my fate,
Creates a spectacle that's hard to debate.

In the corners of calm, boisterous thoughts flow,
Like a garden of giggles that sprouts from below.
With pudding and spoons, the realizations appear,
Each night serves a chuckle as twilight draws near.

So I dance in the shadows, I spin with the breeze,
Here's to the moments where fun is the tease.
An invitation to be, let laughter unfold,
In the embrace of the night, life gleefully told.

Traces of Solitude

In the corner, dust bunnies dance,
They plot my escape, not leaving a chance.
I sip my tea, the cat gives a stare,
As if to say, 'Why do you care?'

The toaster pops, it sounds like a cheer,
Crackers and crumbs, my diet is clear.
I chuckle at socks that have lost their pair,
In solitude's company, I'm blissfully aware.

I gaze out the window, a squirrel on a spree,
Chasing its tail, what a sight to see!
Outside it's a mess, but inside, I thrive,
In my quiet kingdom, I am alive.

When the clock ticks loud, I find it amusing,
Each tock a reminder, life is confusing.
With laughter so near, solitude hugs tight,
In echoes of stillness, I find my delight.

Echoes in the Silence

Whispers of nothing, oh what a sound,
As I shuffle through thoughts that tumble around.
The fridge hums a tune, a ballad so grand,
With leftover pizza, the best in the land.

A chair squeaks softly, it's joined in the fun,
While I ponder why socks always run.
Naps are the treasure, oh what a delight,
In echoes of silence, I bask in the light.

A fly buzzes by, with its aimless ambition,
And I can't help but question its mission.
It lands on the curtain, plays hide-and-seek,
In the calm of my space, I find joy unique.

So here's to the moments, unhurried and free,
With laughter and peace, just my thoughts and me.
With a wink at the chaos that life tends to sow,
I giggle in silence, letting calm take the bow.

A Breath Between Thoughts

Inhale the quiet, exhale the mess,
Each pause a giggle, never a stress.
Coffee's my buddy, in this tranquil scene,
Together we conquer the mundane routine.

With a blink, a thought bounces here and there,
About why I haven't yet combed my hair.
The dog snores softly, a symphony's tune,
As I drift through the day, like a lost balloon.

I ponder the plant that's grown out of sight,
Its mission to thrive in the dead of night.
With mischief in roots, it takes its sweet time,
Turning my boredom into a nursery rhyme.

Each second slinks by, with a chuckle and sigh,
In this dance with stillness, I float, oh so high.
A breath between thoughts, like a hiccup of fun,
In whispers of laughter, I'm never undone.

Reflections on Still Waters

The pond sits placid, like a mirror of cheese,
With ducks that are gossiping, spreading their keys.
They quack about breadcrumbs and who gets the crumbs,
While I contemplate life and the silliness comes.

A lily floats by, with flair and a wink,
It seems to be pondering—what do flowers think?
And as I drift deeper into this absurd,
Nature's the jester, and I'm just a bird.

The clouds overhead, look like cotton candy,
A feast for the eyes, oh so sweet and dandy.
With a splash of a fish, I giggle and sway,
In these quiet moments, I float the day away.

So here in the hush, with no need to jump,
I chuckle at ripples that dance at the lump.
Reflections of laughter on still waters play,
As pure and as silly as a cat on a bay.

In Silence We Discover

In the stillness, socks go missing,
A playful game of hide and seek.
The fridge hums softly, quietly dissing,
While my thoughts wobble, feel so weak.

A goldfish dreams of swimming deep,
In a tank that's quite the snug affair.
I ponder on the secrets I keep,
Staring at bubbles, with a dazed stare.

The cat ponders life, perched on the ledge,
Plotting my doom with a twitch of her tail.
In silence, I sit on the edge,
Wondering if coffee will prevail.

A paused moment, my brain hits a wall,
To-do lists float like balloons in the sky.
Did I forget to call? What was it all?
Perhaps I'll just nap until I know why.

Brushing Against the Subtle

The clock ticks in, a joker it seems,
With every tick, it giggles a bit.
I search for wisdom in half-baked dreams,
While coffee grounds brew a quiet wit.

The dog's snoring sounds like thunder,
As he chases squirrels in the night air.
Spent too much time lost in my blunder,
Yet his sleepy snorts don't seem to care.

Warm cups cradled in gentle hands,
Hold stories brewed with odd flavors.
In subtlety, the world expands,
As I muse over muffin-sweet labors.

Laughter flickers in dust motes above,
The lamp gives a wink, it knows my plight.
In these hush-hush moments, I find love,
Sneaking out giggles from silence's bite.

The Untold Stories of Stillness

Stillness speaks in whispers so sly,
Like a rubber chicken that squeaks at noon.
I spy on nature, oh so spry,
As clouds parade like a loopy cartoon.

My laundry dances in a raucous spin,
With unpaired socks claiming their fame.
In the quiet, however, weird thoughts begin,
Like how must potatoes feel about their name?

A spider weaves tales in silk so fine,
While I ponder pancakes — should I have two?
His eight legs dance, all parts divine,
Inventing ways to make life feel new.

The slice of bread reflects my deep thoughts,
Should I butter it, or leave it plain?
In stories of stillness, my mind plots,
A quest for choco spread — who is to blame?

Illuminated by Solitude

In the morning light, I sip my tea,
Watching the cat chase a shadow, carefree.
A sock on the floor, a glorious sight,
It whispers my name, oh what a delight!

My thoughts wander off like a runaway kite,
To a kitchen dance under fridge's dim light.
I twirl and I leap, for no one can see,
A ballet of one, just the cat and me.

Oh, the fridge hums a tune, quite divine,
As I contemplate where that missing sock might shine.
A squirrel in a tree seems to giggle with glee,
In this moment of quiet, we're all wild and free.

So here in this stillness, a chuckle erupts,
At the dandelion blooms, the lawn's little hiccups.
Life's comics unfold, where I find my delight,
In the small, silly moments, the day is made bright.

The Language of Still Waters

A frog serenades in the pond's gentle hush,
Croaking a tune in the evening's soft blush.
While I find myself lost in this magical breeze,
Wondering if frogs have come to tease.

Leaves rustle softly, as if to confide,
Secrets of nature that patiently bide.
A passing cloud seems to giggle as well,
As I twist in my chair, sharing jokes with the smell.

The water reflects every whimsy and thought,
As I ponder my dinner, oh was it a lot?
The goldfish just snicker, they swim round and round,
In the quiet of dusk, life's humor is found.

So here in this moment, I chuckle and grin,
For the laughter from nature has surely set in.
From frogs to the trees, they all join the fun,
In the humor of silence, we're never outdone.

Nature's Gentle Teachings

A bee in a flower takes the day slow,
Wondering if it's really a pro at the show.
While I ponder life with a grin and a shrug,
Thinking maybe I should just hug a big mug!

The sun dips low, painting skies with a joke,
A squirrel drops acorns, laughs from its cloak.
I join in the laughter, I can't help but chuckle,
At nature's own antics, my curious puzzle.

A breeze carries whispers from leaves overhead,
"What's for dinner?" they murmur, as I scratch my head.
I giggle at daisies trying to bloom,
As if they're the stars in an evening of gloom.

With each passing moment, I find more to cheer,
In the whispers of branches that hover near.
Nature's comedic timing, oh how it plays,
In the gentle of quiet, I smile through the days.

Secrets in the Silence

In the hush of my home, I hear the clock tick,
A symphony of seconds, quite flashy and slick.
Dust bunnies waltz on the floor like mad wits,
While I secretly wish I could take a few hits!

The silence is loud, but it tickles me pink,
As I dwell on my thoughts, more scattered than ink.
Each quiet reflection, a chuckle, a tease,
Like a feather on wind, I go where it pleases.

In the corners, the owls are rolling their eyes,
At all of my ponderings, they plot and devise.
While crickets conspire, their chirps full of cheer,
In the stillness of twilight, they're all laughing here.

So join in the calm, grab a moment to spare,
As laughter in stillness hangs light in the air.
With secrets of silence, oh what a delight,
In the silly, soft moments, everything feels right.

The Calm Before the Clarity

In the stillness, socks go rogue,
A dance of lint, a jester's prologue.
Tea brews slowly, laughing at time,
A spoon's orchestra, a rhythm, a rhyme.

Birds make their sound, a comical chorus,
Chasing their tails, what's so glorious?
The cat eye rolls, it might just be fate,
In this haze, procrastination waits.

Guilt-free napping beneath the sun,
Counting the clouds, just having some fun.
Baking bread that flops on the floor,
The recipe's door remains half open, for sure!

Yet, in this chaos, bubbles arise,
A punchline hidden right before our eyes.
As stillness settles, laughter we chase,
In the calm, we find our hazy grace.

Shadows of Serenity

In shadows where the dust bunnies play,
Lurking around like they've won the day.
Mismatched socks on a chair, what a sight,
They form a crew, plotting their flight!

Sipping tea from a cup that says 'Cheers',
It spills on my shirt while I laugh with my peers.
The plants are judging, or so it seems,
In their quiet stillness, they hatch silly dreams.

There's a pause in the chaos of life's endless race,
Just me, my thoughts, and a cat's furry face.
In twinkling lights, the shadows do prance,
Like a weird magical circus, they dance!

Laughter erupts, surprise at each turn,
While the world spins fast, it's my time to learn.
In silly moments, with humor we bask,
Finding joy is a thrilling task.

Unseen Journeys Within

In the calm, I roam with my snack,
Chips and dip, oh, I've lost track.
Journals half-written, cookies disguised,
In the search for meaning, fun is prioritized.

Between couch cushions, dreams do hide,
A treasure map that's jumbled but wide.
Searching for goals in a nap's embrace,
Who knew success wore a fuzzy face?

The rattle of dishes, what a sweet tune,
Dancing with the dust, in the afternoon.
As laughter bubbles from the kettle's cheer,
My greatest quest is right here, my dear.

Wandering paths of whimsy and glee,
Life's little wonders are waiting for me.
In unseen journeys where silliness reigns,
We embrace the absurd, in laughs where it gains.

Tranquil Reflections

In a puddle's glare, I spot my grin,
Seeing reflections of where I've been.
Pajama days with a book in tow,
Each page a trip to places I know.

Light spills in, nudging me awake,
As my coffee's in danger of taking a break.
I stroll through thoughts, some wear a hat,
Whimsical queries as I giggle at that.

On a rug, I twirl with a snack in hand,
A dance unchoreographed, oh what a stand!
Echoes of laughter in the walls of my mind,
In quiet corners, joyous finds unwind.

With each chuckle, a piece of the day,
In tranquil reflections, I laugh and sway.
Amidst all the chaos, joy truly glows,
In silliness wrapped, life always flows.

Serenity's Soft Embrace

In pajamas of fluffy, I lounge on my chair,
With snacks in my lap, I certainly don't care.
The cat's on the table, he's plotting a scheme,
To steal all my cookies—not part of the dream.

The clock's ticking loudly, but I chill with my tea,
While moments of silence tickle at me.
I ponder the meaning of life and my socks,
As they vanish in laundry—my personal ox.

Days blend like colors in a whimsical haze,
As I drift through my thoughts in a baffling maze.
I muse on the gardens where I might have trod,
But here I am sofa-bound, giving my dog nods.

Oh, serenity's calling with a laugh and a grin,
As I slip into dreams where the real fun begins.
With each quiet chuckle, I sip on my brew,
In the stillness, find joy, who knew it was true?

Navigating the Void

In the depths of my mind, I find treasure and woe,
As I ponder the things I don't want to know.
The fridge hums a tune, a soft serenade,
To the leftover pizza left wilting in shade.

My thoughts take a detour, like a road trip gone wrong,
Where I think of the lyrics to an old catchy song.
I chase after tangents, like clouds in the breeze,
While the world quietly laughs at my whims and my tease.

I set sail in stillness on a sea made of thoughts,
Where the fish are my choices, the net is my knots.
But with waves of distraction, I'm tossed to and fro,
In the void, there's a joke in the calm undertow.

As the silence composes a symphony bright,
I discover my laughter, a soft burst of light.
In the maze of my mind, what a ride it can be,
Navigating the void is less scary—ah, me!

Threads of Thought in Stillness

Once I tried knitting, thought it'd help me unwind,
But I tangled these threads, now the yarn's intertwined.
A needle's a weapon when chaos ensues,
In the stillness of silence, I've nothing to lose.

I ponder my next meal, should I fry or should bake,
But pizza's a promise I seldom forsake.
I stretch out my body, with dreams from my chair,
As the world keeps on spinning, I'm floating on air.

I sip on my drink while lost in a daze,
Where my thoughts flutter softly like leaves in a maze.
Each thread of my pondering weaves tales of delight,
In the quietest moments, my giggles take flight.

Tickle my funny bone, as the clock chimes a tune,
In the stillness, I frolic with thoughts like a loon.
For the magic of stillness, it tickles and bends,
With laughter and wonder, my quicksilver friends.

The Beauty of Breathing Slow

With a yawn and a stretch, I embrace the day's light,
A slow-motion dance where nothing feels right.
I breathe in the comfort of cozy's embrace,
As I revel in moments—a giggly sweet space.

The toaster pops loudly, a startled refrain,
As I question my choices while sipping champagne.
Each bubble's a whisper, a tickle, a tease,
And I chuckle at how life can be such a breeze.

In the art of the slow, there's a giddy delight,
Where I ponder my future and laugh through the night.
Like turtles in leisure, we wander through time,
In the beauty of breathing, we giggle and rhyme.

So let's toast to the silence, the puns and the fun,
As we bask in the beauty; we've only begun.
In the stillness, we twirl, and how sweetly we flow,
For the chuckles of life are a reason to glow!

The Quiet Dance of Dreams

In the still of night, my socks take flight,
Twisting and twirling, what a silly sight.
My cat joins in, with a flick of her tail,
Together we waltz, the ultimate fail.

The fridge starts humming a tune so sweet,
My sandwich is dancing, what a treat!
With peanut butter steps and jelly sways,
We groove in the kitchen like it's a café.

The shadows chuckle, playing peek-a-boo,
As I trip on a shoe, and laugh at the view.
The socks do the cha-cha, the bread twists around,
In this wacky ball, joy is what's found.

So let's boogie on soft floors, with lighthearted tunes,
Embracing the goofiness beneath the moons.
In the dance of dreams, every giggle ignites,
The silly, sweet moments, our hearts take flight.

Interludes of Reflection

Amidst my thoughts, a cactus appeared,
With prickles of wisdom, I'm mildly cheered.
I pondered its pointy, zesty embrace,
And chuckled at life's odd, prickly race.

A sock puppet chimes in with sage advice,
"Life's but a stage, don't take it too nice!"
With fabric hands waving, it starts to preach,
About finding value in what's out of reach.

I sip from my mug of lukewarm regret,
While pondering dance moves I can't quite perfect.
The mirror just laughs, a reflective ally,
As I shimmy and swirl, quite the goofy guy!

So here's to the laughs hidden under our hats,
To giggles and grins and wise pillow chats.
In quiet moments, the madness does blend,
Creating a symphony where humor won't end.

The Heart Finds its Rhythm

While wandering lonely, a beat drops near,
A squirrel shakes its tail, brings laughter and cheer.
His acorn-sized heart conducts the parade,
I can't help but giggle at the antics displayed.

With each little pause, my thoughts start to jig,
The world spins around like a bright, bouncy jig.
I tripped on a shoelace, rolled in a knot,
Yet laughter erupts from the mess that I've shot.

In the chaos of silence where giggles reside,
I dance with the daydreams that wiggle inside.
An imaginary band plays a tune so spry,
As I twirl on my toes, the clouds dance by.

So let's cradle the chuckles, let rhythms take flight,
In the heart of the hush, where laughter feels right.
The whispers of joy, like a breeze on the run,
In moments of calm, life's melody is spun.

Breathing in Solitary Spaces

In a bubble of quiet, I fill up with air,
A rubber chicken clucks and shakes off despair.
It struts like a peacock, so proud, so bright,
As I ponder my thoughts in the still of the night.

The crickets serenade with chirps all around,
While I sip my tea on this crooked mound.
The puddles reflect each wobble and sway,
And laughter erupts as I dress like a ray.

I practice my yoga upon a whoopee mat,
Each pose brings a chuckle—what's this? A spat!
Just me and the humor of clumsiness sweet,
Beneath starlit giggles, my world feels complete.

In moments of solitude, where silliness hums,
I find life's been bursting with joy and with puns.
So here's to the breezes that bubble in place,
In solitary spaces, I wear my joy's face.

The Deep Breath of Dawn

The sun yawns wide, but I'm still asleep,
My coffee's brewing, a secret to keep.
The cat sits plotting, a grand little scheme,
While I chase my thoughts in a caffeine dream.

The toast pops up like it's waving hello,
With butter and jam, a breakfast show.
The clock hands dance, but I'm in a trance,
With crumbs on my shirt, who said I can't prance?

Birds gossip softly, under the trees,
While squirrels are dodging those awkward bees.
In these little moments, I do a jig,
Who knew the dawn held such joy in a fig?

So here I sit, in morning's embrace,
Between bites of muffins, I find my place.
Laughing at shadows that stretch on the floor,
In the dawn's quiet giggle, who could ask for more?

Heartbeats in the Hush

In the still of the night, the fridge hums a tune,
Like a concert hall, beneath the pale moon.
The cat thinks it's hunting at three in the dark,
While I half-heartedly pretend to be a shark.

The clock ticks louder than a marching band,
With echoes of dreams I won't understand.
A sock on the floor, the dog gives a stare,
Like 'why are you up? Go bathe in despair!'

Yet here in the quiet, a giggle does bloom,
I swat at the shadows while sweeping the gloom.
For every heartbeat, I chuckle and sigh,
Embracing the nonsense, allowing it to fly.

So let the world spin with its chaotic flair,
I'll dance with the silence; I'll still have my share.
With laughter and mischief in this midnight hush,
I find my delight in a playful, sweet rush.

Subtle Wonders of the Ordinary

The spoon in the drawer gave a clatter today,
As I hunted for snacks in a gluttonous way.
The chair let out groans like an old man's sigh,
In the symphony of life, it's my time to fly.

The dust on the shelf isn't just old and grey,
It's confetti from parties that went far astray.
I laugh at the laundry, a mountain so high,
Like I'm climbing Everest, oh me, oh my!

The fridge has a magnet that's lost every fight,
And I giggle as I stumble, quite lacking in grace.
But laughter's the spice that we sprinkle on life,
In moments of chaos, we find what's right.

So here's to the small things that make me smile wide,
To socks full of holes and the crumbs that abide.
Each day is a treasure, packed tight with delight,
In the ordinary's charm, we take happy flight.

Essence of a Moments' Peace

A teacup sits waiting, like a friend in the storm,
With steam dancing freely, its shape going warm.
A cookie does wobble, it feebly contests,
But I'll eat with a smirk, I'm truly obsessed.

The chair creaks beneath me, a solid old star,
Each squeak a reminder that we've come so far.
I sip and I munch, a delicious charade,
While the world tries to hustle, I'm blissfully laid.

The curtains are fluttering, gossiping low,
Over tales of the morning, the sun's warm glow.
A critter sneaks by on a picturesque quest,
With no care for deadlines, it's just feeling blessed.

So here's to each moment that wraps me so tight,
In the warmth of my nook, the chaos feels right.
With laughter in silence, we twirl in delight,
In the essence of peace, life's the best kind of light.

Melodies of Silent Affection

In a world where chaos reigns,
I hum my songs of lazy gains.
While socks are lost, the cat's a queen,
In this sweet mess, life's a routine.

Cup of tea on the side, I grin,
The crumbs of cookies, my little sin.
The sound of silence? A hearty laugh,
Amidst piled laundry, my favorite path.

Ripples of Restful Thought

The clock tick-tocks, but who's in a race?
I find deep wisdom in this slow pace.
Couch potato, I eat popcorn,
Philosopher of crumbs, not forlorn.

My brain's a circus, but you already knew,
Juggling thoughts with a chip, it's true.
Amidst the stillness, I laugh and boast,
Dreaming big while I nap—what a host!

Lightness in the Slow Hour

In the quiet, my mind starts to roam,
With pie on my lap, I call it home.
Thoughts dance like dust in the sun's bright beam,
As I ponder life, or maybe ice cream.

Each moment whispers its silly refrain,
Like a cat in repose, who feels no pain.
With a chuckle I sip, let the drivel flow,
In stillness, I find joy in the show.

When Solitude Speaks

Alone I stand, with a muffin's might,
In solitude's grip, I feel alright.
Conversations with my snack so grand,
A sugary chat that's simply unplanned.

The couch knows all my secrets and dreams,
As I ponder life's odd, quirky schemes.
With a wink at the clock, I sit with glee,
And let tick-tock time set my thoughts free.

Still Waters Run Deep

In the stillness, my thoughts wander,
Like a cat chasing shadows, soft and fonder.
A sock goes missing, oh what a crime,
Is it a portal? Or just laundry's prime?

I brew my tea, with leaves that dance,
As I ponder life, in a wistful trance.
Did I just hear my sandwich call?
Or was it the fridge, just wanting to brawl?

Outside, the birds are throwing a bash,
While my mind's busy in a whimsical clash.
What's the meaning of toast burned too dark?
Is it art, or just my inner spark?

In these moments, I laugh with glee,
Life's oddities are a comedy spree.
Who knew the quiet could be so bold?
Hiding mysteries just waiting to unfold?

Tranquil Horizons

As the sun dips low, I start to think,
About dinner's fate, and the kitchen's stink.
Do I risk the curry, now on the verge?
Or just order pizza and let cravings surge?

The clouds parade in fluffy delight,
I chase my daydreams, like a nosy kite.
What would happen if I joined a band?
Or tried to juggle with a solid hand?

My thoughts meander, like a stray dog,
While I debate with a tasting fog.
Should I waltz or should I hop?
Decisions become a bubbling pop!

In this calm, silliness takes the reins,
Whispers of laughter through my veins.
Life's too short to fret or be terse,
So I toast to quirkiness and the universe!

Silent Conversations with the Soul

In silence, I ask, where'd my keys go?
Is my brain a sieve, or is it just so?
Pondering my lunch like a secret vault,
Is it leftovers, or a culinary assault?

The cat gives me judgment, oh so sly,
Does it care if I bake or just buy pie?
With purring wisdom, it stares and grooms,
Maybe it knows the best kitchen blooms!

Floating thoughts land like leaves in fall,
Do squirrels have purpose? Or dreams at all?
What if their nests are like tiny hotels?
And they gossip about nuts and savory spells?

So here I sit, sipping from a cup,
While pondering life and the last hiccup.
In these quiet moments, laughter ignites,
Turning mundanity into wonders and flights.

The Pause that Refreshes

With a pause, I reflect on my shopping spree,
Did I really need five kinds of tea?
Now my cupboard's bursting, a blend so grand,
Next week's scone fest—oh, life's unplanned!

I sit on the couch, a true noble rest,
Remote in hand, I dream of my quest.
How many sitcoms will inspire a goal?
Or lead me astray like a runaway shoal?

A spider spins webs while my mind takes flight,
In the battle of chaos and calm, I write.
Does the broom know it's the brush of fate?
Or just knows to sweep when it's getting late?

These pauses are fragrant, like cake in the air,
A giggle at life's odd, delightful affair.
So here's to the stillness, oddly profound,
In quietest moments, humor abounds!

Notes from the Silent Symphony

In a world where chatter takes the stage,
I sit with socks that don't quite match.
They hum a tune, just for me,
As I sip my tea, not quite a catch.

The kettle's song is pure delight,
While the cat naps in a sunlit beam.
My thoughts dance like spaghetti on a plate,
Twisting and turning, a noodle dream.

Every tick of the clock, a giggle hides,
As I ponder why toast always lands buttered side down.
Invisible giggling ghosts pass by,
Whispering secrets that wear a frown.

In the still of the day, with a grin so wide,
I chase my thoughts, they run like squirrels.
Who needs an audience for a show this grand?
Just me and my coffee, and the world twirls.

The Weight of Wandering Thoughts

Thoughts parade in a conga line,
Stumbling over mossy rocks and dreams.
Why do I think of dancing llamas?
Life's not always as it seems.

In the middle of a serious chat,
Why does my mind predict a pie?
As it floats off to distant lands,
I can't help but laugh and sigh.

A suitcase packed with hopes and fears,
It weighs a ton but feels so light.
I ponder how to sneak in a nap,
As my wandering thoughts take flight.

In the quiet corners of my mind,
Hiccups of laughter bubble up.
Knitting together tales so odd,
Who knew daydreams could be a cup?

Lanterns of Quiet Influence

In the nook of a chair, I sit and think,
Lanterns flicker like my runaway mind.
Why do socks disappear, dear universe?
Are they plotting? Am I blind?

A bubble of silence wraps around,
While my brain tosses confetti high.
Thoughts trip over themselves with grace,
Chasing butterflies, oh my, oh my!

A sudden urge for a cupcake treat,
With sprinkles that dance like little stars.
My inner voice shouts, 'What a delight!'
While the world forgets my breakfast bars.

In this cozy cocoon, I behave like a fool,
Dancing with echoes in slippers worn
Maybe the charm is just this giggle,
Among quiet lanterns, I'm reborn.

When the World Holds Its Breath

When silence drapes like a cozy quilt,
And the world stops on its usual grind,
I hear the laughter of books on shelves,
Whispering jokes that are one of a kind.

A lone squirrel steals my sandwich plan,
While I ponder the meaning of jelly beans.
Why is babbling a favorite pastime?
As I juggle my thoughts like ice cream machines.

In the pause of a sneeze, I find some peace,
Who knew quiet moments could tickle so bright?
With a snicker, I stumble on puns so fresh,
As the world holds its breath, all feels just right.

Standing on clouds made of marshmallow fluff,
I dance through the stillness, a comical show.
Maybe the quiet is where we should be,
Where chuckles roll in and mischief can glow.

Serenity's Subtle Call

In the stillness, socks go rogue,
Dancers twirl on floors of fog.
Lost in thought, I munch on fries,
While my cat perfects her spy disguise.

Tea spills like wisdom in the air,
Who knew spills could spark such flair?
A dusty book hints at a quest,
Only to find it's just a jest.

A whisper floats on winds so mild,
A dance with shadows, oh so wild.
Yet all I seek in the softest hum,
Is the last cookie I can nibble and succumb.

In every pause, a chuckle brews,
In laughter's cloak, I lose my blues.
Amid silence, my giggles grow,
Like popcorn popping, watch them flow!

Moments of Unspoken Grace

A quiet moment in the chair,
I contemplate the spaghetti in my hair.
What's the meaning of a soggy noodle?
Perhaps it's art that's gone a little poodle.

The clock ticks loud, yet the cat's got a plan,
To catch a sunbeam, or so he can.
I sip my tea—what a crucial sip,
And find my thoughts take a delightful trip.

A small pet rock rolls beneath my feet,
Whispering secrets from an ancient street.
If rocks can dream, what do they see?
A world where they're better, just like me!

Every quiet giggle, each stifled snort,
Brings treasures of joy, in my little court.
Here's to moments, both silly and sweet,
Where laughter finds rhythm, and life feels complete!

Undercurrents of Reflection

In still waters where ripples play,
I ponder if ducks have anything to say.
They glide with purpose, or so they seem,
While I contemplate my lunchtime dream.

A squirrel scurries, with acorns to stash,
In the quiet glow of the afternoon dash.
Am I the squirrel, or just a nut?
Either way, the world's a fun little rut.

Pondering life while my toast burns black,
I wonder if my toaster thinks I lack.
But every char speaks of time well spent,
Each crispy edge, my little event.

In the hush, my thoughts dance and twirl,
Like balloons at a wedding, they spin and swirl.
The magic's in laughter, the antics we weave,
In the cozy chaos, we learn to believe!

The Language of Quietude

While the world whirs with a bustling tune,
I find solace in the glow of the moon.
What secrets hide in nighttime's embrace?
Perhaps it's just confusion on my face.

A rubber chicken sits with poise,
Telling jokes in the silence noise.
What wisdom lies in a plastic beak?
A giggle of truth, or a ticklish peek?

In the quiet, I'll swing like a breeze,
With daydreams floating among the trees.
A butterfly's sneeze might break the calm,
To which I'd respond, "That's quite the charm!"

In whimsical quiet, life's essence flows,
Through odd thoughts and snickering prose.
May we embrace the humor unseen,
In the gentle moments, where we're all keen!

Harmony in the Hush

In the stillness, the fridge starts to hum,
My thoughts gather like a marching drum.
Socks on the floor play a violin tune,
As I sit in the quiet—who knew it was a boon?

Spiders spin webs, weaving tales untold,
In corners they dance, so brave and so bold.
The cat lounges deep, dreaming wildly of fish,
While I sip on tea, and accomplish my wish.

Whispers of dust float in the gentle light,
Reminding me surely that life's not a fight.
The clock softly ticks, a comical beat,
As I wade through my thoughts, in my fuzzy house feet.

In the quietness found, there's laughter and glee,
Like finding a button that's lost in the sea.
A moment of pause, how silly and grand,
In a world that rushes, we now understand!

The Canvas of Contemplation

A paintbrush of silence creates all around,
As I ponder the wonders that quietly abound.
A potato on the counter is pondering fate,
Should it be mashed, or just lie there and wait?

The goldfish is swimming with movements so sleek,
While I write my thoughts down, feeling quite chic.
A sneezing match starts with the dust in the air,
Each sneeze is a giggle, I just can't compare.

Clouds drift by slowly like cream on my tea,
I watch them intently—it's just so carefree!
The daydreams I gather, like socks in a pile,
Bring a chuckle to my face, it's all worth the while.

So here in this moment, humor and whim,
The world seems a canvas, a life on a whim.
Brush stokes of silence, in laughter we swipe,
Creating a masterpiece with each little type.

Tranquil Embrace of the Now

The couch whispers softly, I've reached my new throne,
Am I watching a show, or just scrolling alone?
A slight giggle erupts as I nibble on chips,
Crunching my way through these calm little trips.

The clock has a joke, tick-tock, what a clown,
It tells me it's time to just sit and look down.
The cat gives me side-eye, an expert in chill,
While I ponder my snacks and the couch's great thrill.

Curtains wave gently, a breeze on my cheek,
A rhythm of laughter flows soft and unique.
The plants hold a dance party, leaves all aglow,
While I sip on my coffee, soaked in the flow.

In this tranquil embrace, hilarity blooms,
Where silence is gold and joy fully looms.
We find that the quiet can tickle the brain,
In moments of now, life's pretty insane!

The Secret Life of Pauses

In the pauses of life there's a giggle they weave,
Like secrets of socks when we want to believe.
A teapot whistles tunes that could make you dance,
As I ponder the wonders of my old sweatpants.

The banana speaks softly, 'Eat me, I dare!'
While my toast pops up, like it's dressed for a fair.
Uneaten leftovers, revolution ignites,
They plot in the fridge for memorable nights.

A pause in my thoughts brings a chuckle so sweet,
Like slipping on slippers that are two left feet.
The humor in silence swirls round like a sprite,
As I bask in the joy of a lazy delight.

Here's to the moments when laughter takes charge,
In the pause of a breath, life feels rather large.
So let's tiptoe through stillness, embrace every grin,
For the secret of pauses is where we begin!

The Art of Being Still

In the midst of every flurry,
Sitting still can seem quite furry.
A squirrel scampers, leaves a trace,
While I sip tea and mock the race.

Minutes stretch like slimy dough,
My thoughts bounce fast, then run too slow.
I ponder pizza, plots, and plans,
While outside, chaos rules like fans.

Yet in this pause, I snag a thought,
Should I really dance or just eat rot?
The fridge hums softly, sings a tune,
As I embrace this lovely swoon.

So here's my art, I dawdle with flair,
In stillness, the nutty squirrels declare:
Life is best when you take a break,
And maybe toss a nut for fate's sake!

Gentle Murmurs of Dawn

When dawn creeps in, I'm wrapped in dreams,
While birds debate their early themes.
Caffeine calls with a gentle shout,
But sleepyheads are still about.

A sock wonky, my coffee's cold,
The sun creeps up, feeling quite bold.
The world goes wild, yet here I sit,
Half-clothed and calm, embracing wit.

Morning whispers tickle my ears,
While I juggle cereal and fears.
But in this dance of spoons and cups,
The calm brings giggles, filled with ups.

So let the roosters wail away,
I'll commune with crumbs, and softly sway.
In gentle murmurs, I'll find my heart,
In the chaos, I'll play my part!

In the Embrace of Calm

A cat stretches wide, in relaxed bliss,
While I ponder my next snack, oh what a risk!
With calm in the air, I might just lie,
And channel my inner lazy pie.

Time slows down, like melted cheese,
I contemplate life, and what truly frees.
Laundry waits, and plants need care,
But here I am, floating in mid-air.

Angry dandelions knock at the door,
While I giggle at them, funny lore.
My slippers squeak, a cozy little song,
As I sit here thinking, what's right or wrong?

So, in this embrace of mellow vibes,
I'll nurture quirks, and twirl my jibes.
For stillness is where the laughter blooms,
Among the socks and dust, in quiet rooms!

Soft Footfalls on Silent Paths

In the hush, my feet do dance,
On silent paths, I take a chance.
With every step, a giggle slips,
As I dodge the grass and clumsy trips.

The squirrels chime in, with chatter loud,
While I'm lost in thoughts, feeling proud.
Each soft footfall whispers a tune,
Of harmonic mishaps and spoons out at noon.

Butterflies strut while I'm stuck on grass,
And wonder if this moment will pass.
With every pause, I just might see,
The riotous laugh that sets me free.

So here I wander, lounging with grace,
In soft footfalls, I find my space.
With jokes of nature, I explore and grin,
In this rhythmic roam, where stillness begins!

Moments Cradled in Calm

In the chair where the dust bunnies play,
I ponder the meaning of yesterday's hay.
A sock on the floor, a rogue spoon in sight,
I chuckle at life, in this quiet twilight.

The cat curls up like a burrito bold,
Dreaming of fish that he never quite told.
I sip my tea, the world fades away,
In the calm of the moment, I laugh and stay.

My to-do list is missing, or possibly lost,
To the depths of the couch, an abyss, not a cost.
I find joy in pauses, in laughter, in breath,
As life quietly whispers, "There's fun beyond death."

So here in my calm, a new venture begins,
Maybe I'll dance, or just muse about sins.
For in each silent heartbeat, humor does swell,
Amidst the madness, I chuckle quite well.

The Wisdom of Watching Clouds

Lying on grass, embracing the blue,
I see a giant sandwich, not one, but a few.
The clouds drift by with a leisurely grace,
Laughing at life's never-ending race.

A fluffy dog sits, thinking hard, you see,
About how to catch the squirrel up a tree.
While I wonder if jellybeans float in the sky,
Or if wishes come true, if you really try.

Shapes shift and shimmer, a whale or a shoe,
My imagination's wild, and it knows what to do.
So I wave to the clouds, with a wink and a grin,
Who'd have thought such wisdom could linger within?

And when it rains suddenly, I just splash and play,
For the clouds write their stories in a fabulous way.
With each droplet dancing, a joke's in the air,
Life's punchline is here, if you simply dare.

Whispers of the Heart

In the silence, my heart begins to hum,
With rhythms of laughter, it beats like a drum.
I sit with my thoughts, a parade of sorts,
Where giggles collide with philosophical sports.

I overhear squirrels plotting their schemes,
While birds write ballads about silly dreams.
A leaf falls down, like a graceful ballet,
To remind me that joy doesn't fade away.

A napkin confesses its love for a pen,
As crumbs dance around like they've found new friends.
In this quiet, I witness the odd and the sweet,
A comedy show in my own humble seat.

So cheers to the giggles within every sigh,
The whispers of hearts, and the truth in the sky.
For life is just richer when chuckled at best,
In laughter, we find what we treasure, the quest.

The Stillness Speaks

In the stillness, I notice a snail on his quest,
Journeying slowly, with no need to invest.
A cookie crumbles, and my heart skips a beat,
As the snail gives a shrug, 'Life's also a treat.'

The clock ticks away, a gentle reminder,
That time's but a joke, a playful finder.
While I sip my cocoa, and ponder the scene,
What if the world is simply a meme?

The plants in the corner are plotting a dance,
While I look on astonished, missing my chance.
A moment of stillness, a giggle breaks through,
Even nature enjoys a fine comedic view.

So here in the pause, the laughter unfurls,
As the quiet surrounds me, and joy gently swirls.
The stillness may whisper secrets of light,
But in every soft chuckle, it's all just right.

www.ingramcontent.com/pod-product-compliance
Lightning Source LLC
Chambersburg PA
CBHW051655160426
43209CB00004B/900